MW01094468

THE GOLDFIELD HOTEL

Gem of the Desert

by
Patty Cafferata

Eastern Slope
• PUBLISHER •

Reno, Nevada

THE GOLDFIELD HOTEL: GEM OF THE DESERT

Second Edition, index added. Copyright ©2004, ©2005,
by Patricia D. Cafferata.
All rights reserved. No part of this book may be used
or reproduced in any manner whatsoever
without prior permission from the publisher.

Book and Cover design by Pietra Brady

ISBN 0-9746996-1-6
Eastern Slope Publisher
P.O. Box 20357
Reno, Nevada 89515-0357
Printed in the United States of America

ACKNOWLEDGEMENTS

Special thanks to the following people who made this book possible: Elisa Maser for her suggestions and editorial assistance; Pietra Brady for her creative design; Guy Rocha, Assistant Administrator, Nevada State Archives and Records, for his recommendations on Goldfield history; Allen Metscher, Central Nevada historian, for his suggestions on Goldfield history; Mella Harmon, Nevada Historic Preservation Specialist, for her information on Goldfield architecture and the National Register; Eva La Rue, Assistant Curator of the Central Nevada Museum for her assistance on photographs of Goldfield; Lee Brumbaugh, Curator of Photography, and Eric Moody, Curator of Manuscripts, Nevada Historical Society, for their assistance with the photographs and research on the Goldfield Hotel; the staff of Karen Scott, Esmeralda County Recorder, Jim Paulis and Lois Skullestad for their research of the Esmeralda County records; Ben Viljoen, Chair of the Esmeralda County Commission for his suggestions.

The information in this book was collected from sources at the Nevada Historical Society, the Central Nevada Museum and the Esmeralda County Recorder's office. The information was found in local and state newspaper articles in *The Goldfield News*, *Daily Nevada State Journal*, *Goldfield Daily Tribune*, *Goldfield Chronicle*, *Lovelock Review-Miner*, *Reno Evening Gazette*, *Goldfield News & Weekly Tribune*, *Nevada State Journal*, *Las Vegas Sun*, *Eagle Standard*, *Western Nevada Dispatch*, *Las Vegas Review Journal*, and *Nevada Appeal*. And, the *S.F. Examiner & Chronicle* was the source of information on Arthur Trevor's myths about the Goldfield Hotel.

The following books contained background information on Goldfield and the hotel: *Goldfield* by Hugh Shamberger; *George Wingfield: Owner and Operator of Nevada* by C. Elizabeth Raymond; *The Ignoble Conspiracy: Radicalism on Trial in Nevada* by Sally Zanjani and Guy Rocha; *Nevada's Twentieth-Century Mining Boom: Tonopah, Goldfield, Ely* by Russell Elliott; *Goldfield: The Last Gold Rush on the Western Frontier* by Sally Zanjani; *But You Can't Leave, Shirley* by Shirley Porter; *Nevada: A Narrative of the Conquest of a Frontier Land* by James Scrugham, Editor, Vol. II; *Nevada Biographies; Who's Who in Nevada: Biographical Directory of Men and Women Who Are Building Our State*, Vol.1, 1931-1932.

Finally, additional information was obtained from the Wingfield papers at the Nevada Historical Society and articles in the *Central Nevada's Glorious Past*, a publication of the Central Nevada Historical Society.

⇒ GEM OF THE DESERT ⇐

A REPORTER from the *Goldfield Daily Times* dubbed the Goldfield Hotel the "gem of the desert' when it opened in 1908. While the Goldfield Hotel is a historic gem today, it has not proven to be a treasure to its many owners. The hotel was built on the hope that the gold mining boom would continue for years. The population surged to between 20,000 and 25,000 people. The legislature recognized the shift in population and moved the Esmeralda County seat from Hawthorne to Goldfield. The change officially took place on May 1, 1907.

Unfortunately, the high grade gold ore in the area was depleted shortly after the hotel opened its doors to the people flocking to town to seek their fortunes.

Frances Mohawk high grade gold ore worth $750,000 deposited in the State Bank.
-- *Nevada Historical Society*

The mining boom was over by 1910, even though mining activities continued until 1916. In total, the mines produced more than $85 million. When the gold was mined out, the town population rapidly declined as did the hotel's worth. It has been closed for more than 50 years.

The hotel faces Columbia Street on the corner of Crook

Street in the center of Goldfield, Nevada in the middle of the Goldfield National Register Historic District. Goldfield is on U.S. Highway 95, approximately 170 miles north of Las Vegas and 265 miles south of Reno.

The magnificent building sits proudly in the center of town dwarfing the dusty, unpainted insignificant buildings, stores, houses and weed-filled vacant lots around

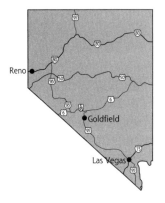

it. Some of the other substantial buildings in town are the Esmeralda Courthouse, Firehouse, and high school, a few blocks east of the hotel, and the Nixon Wingfield and the Curtis-Ish buildings, one block north of the hotel. The Goldfield Hotel has weathered nearly a century of financial tragedy, never living up to the golden dreams of its owners.

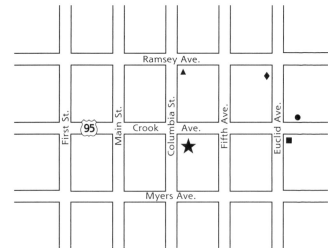

★ **Goldfield Hotel**

● Esmeralda County Courthouse

▲ Nixon Wingfield and Curtis-Ish buildings

■ Goldfield Firehouse

◆ High School

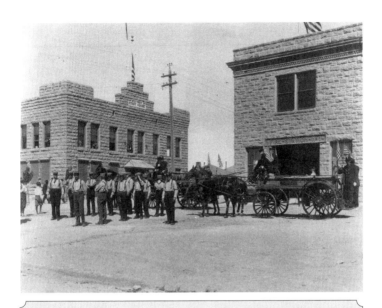

Fire Station No. 1 of the Goldfield Fire Department. The station was completed in August 1908. The Esmeralda County Courthouse opened the same year (although the headstone on the building states 1907, the year construction of the building began) is in the background. -- *Nevada Historical Society*

Goldfield Hotel on the corner of Crook and Columbia Streets.
-- *Frances Crumley Collection*

❦ GOLDFIELD HAS QUIET BEGINNING ❧

THE RUSH TO GOLDFIELD, NEVADA was triggered by the location of three gold claims in the Grandpa Mining District on Columbia Mountain on December 4, 1902.
Prospectors Harry Stimler and William Marsh named the claims the "May Queen," the "Sandstorm," and the "Kruger." They were

Panorama of Goldfield, Nevada with Columbia Mountain in the background.

grubstaked by Jim Butler and Tom Kendall. Apparently, the prospectors were in no hurry to advertise their claims because they did not record them at Hawthorne, then the Esmeralda County seat, until March 4, 1903. Stimler and Marsh did not stop mining after their initial discoveries. They remained in the area and recorded numerous other claims.

Stimler and Marsh and other early prospectors used burros as pack animals, and the teamsters used burros to haul the ore from the mines to the mills. These animals were a common sight in the Goldfield area before the advent of the automobile. Today, a band of wild burros is often spotted on the west side of U.S. Highway 95 between Tonopah and Goldfield.

At the time of the gold discovery, the Goldfield area was federal land. Evidently, this fact did not bother the miners or mining companies that flocked to the area. The Goldfield townsite was surveyed by Elmer Chute of the Goldfield Land and Development Company in September 1903. Based on his map, his company auctioned off town lots creating the first rush to Goldfield. The purchasers of the lots were essentially squatters because Chute's company did not have title to the lands they were selling. Soon after the initial town lots were sold, a post office was established, a public school was opened, and a volunteer fire department was organized.

Bill Marsh. Marsh and Harry Stimler were the original prospectors to stake three gold claims on Columbia Mountain in what later became Goldfield, Nevada. -- *Nevada Historical Society*

Harry Stimler with his boys. Stimler was boyhood friends with Bill Marsh, the other prospector who discovered the original gold claims on Columbia Mountain in what later became Goldfield, Nevada. Stimler's mother was Native American; some reports state she was a Paiute, others state she was a Shoshone. -- *Nevada Historical Society*

Teamsters in downtown Goldfield. -- *Nevada Historical Society*

CURRENT HOTEL BUILDING WAS NOT THE FIRST HOTEL

THIS LANDMARK HOTEL was not the first Goldfield Hotel. There were two other hotels in the same location on Columbia between Crook and Myers streets that burned down before the current magnificent stone and brick structure was built.

The first hotel was built sometime before the major fire on July 8, 1905. The fire started in the Bon Ton Millinery store located in the same block as the hotel. That fire quickly consumed the entire block of buildings, including the hotel. The fire damage to the hotel was estimated to be $35,000.

In 1906, the big bonanza was hit on the Hayes and Monette lease on the Mohawk No. 2 claim. This discovery marked the beginning of the big rush to Goldfield. One of the newcomers included George Wingfield, who later dominated the mining, financial, and political spheres of the town and the State of Nevada. His success and wealth came not only from his ownership of the Goldfield Consolidated Mines Company, but also from other investments around the state.

Wingfield derrick. -- *Nevada Historical Society*

Wingfield was not the only prominent man to prosper in Goldfield. To promote the town and further investments in the area, Tex Rickard, Ben Rosenthal, George Graham Rice and others arranged the Gans-Nelson lightweight world title fight in September 1906. It was reported that about 7,000 people flocked to Goldfield to watch the fight in an arena constructed specifically for the fight.

Gans-Nelson fight on September 3, 1906. Joe Gans is on the right. Oscar "Battling" Nelson is on the left. The lightweight championship fight was promoted by saloon keeper George Lewis "Tex" Rickard, George Graham Rice and Ben Rosenthal to showcase Goldfield and their mining stocks. The match lasted 42 rounds when Nelson deliberately threw a punch below Gans' belt. The judge disqualified Nelson and awarded the victory to Gans.
-- *Nevada Historical Society*

After 42 rounds, "Battling" Nelson lost by throwing a low blow which the referee called a foul, so the champion, Joe Gans, kept his title. According to their agreement before the fight, Nelson received twice as much of the approximate $30,000 purse as Gans received.

Meanwhile, a new hotel was under construction to replace the one destroyed by the fire. The new building was a two story wooden structure with electric lights throughout the building of more than fifty rooms that opened in October 1905, and was known as the Hotel Goldfield. The owner, G.M. Harris, paid about $30,000 to J.E. Bundy to build the

Hotel Goldfield in 1905. -- *Nevada Historical Society*

structure and spent another $8,000 on furnishings. It was one of the largest structures in the city when it opened.

Harris' ads claimed the hotel was comfortable and luxurious and boasted that the sleeping apartments would be supplied with hot and cold running water, and private baths were attached to some of the rooms. The hotel featured a 38 foot by 32 foot office with a bar attached, and a large sample room for traveling salesmen to display their wares. The owners assured the public that the facility was equipped with numerous, conveniently located fire escapes offering safe exits from the building. Sadly, this claim proved false.

Apparently, Harris did not open this hotel. He could not make his mortgage payments to the State Bank and Trust Company. In February 1906, the bank's attorney, John Franklin (Frank) Douglas, bought part interest in the hotel. A native of Franktown, Nevada, he graduated from the University of

California at Berkeley with an engineering degree, and he read the law in California. He arrived in Goldfield to open his law practice in 1905.

A Republican, he was appointed district attorney in May 1906, but he lost the general election in November 1906. Douglas was hired as special prosecutor in the murder case filed against Morrie Preston and Joseph Smith, alleged union activists. That trial began in April 1907.

In October 1906, Douglas was the person to actually open the second Hotel Goldfield. The next month, the Goldfield Realty Company became the owners of the property. The corporation was created on November 14, 1906 and filed its Articles of Incorporation on December 12, 1906. In addition to Douglas, the original shareholders of the company were: G.H. Hayes and Al Myers, of Los Angeles, California; Harry Benedict and John Smith of Chicago, Illinois (Benedict and Smith were the original backers of the Hayes- Monette lease); and James R. Davis and M.J. Monette. Apparently, they each owned 25,000 shares of the corporation, except for Douglas who owned 15,000 shares.

There were plans to add a restaurant at an estimated cost of $16,000 and an annex to the hotel with an additional 45 bedrooms, 10 of which were to have bathrooms and radiator heat. The cost of constructing the annex was estimated to be $20,000.

The new owners of the hotel awarded builders Waugh and Henningson a $16,000 contract to build a new one-story restaurant building adjoining the hotel. On November 17, 1906, less than a month after the second Hotel Goldfield opened, another fire swept through Goldfield in the early morning destroying the entire hotel, the unfinished restaurant and annex buildings.

Newspaper reports are conflicting; either the fire was started by live wires on the hotel's roof or by a defective flue on the second floor. There were more than 70 guests in the hotel and some of them broke their legs or ankles jumping from the upper story windows or sustained other injuries from the smoke and the fire. Tragically, two guests perished in the fire: Judge J. M. Ellis of the Marshall-Ellis Investment Company from Denver, Colorado, and A.H. Hever, investment broker, of Los Angeles, California.

The exact loss on the property was unknown. According to the newspaper reports, the owners collected between $18,000 - $30,000 from their insurance company on the buildings. Losses not covered by insurance were anywhere from $40,000 - $140,000.

THE GOLDFIELD HOTEL

THE MOST MODERN HOTEL IN NEVADA
Constructed at a cost of $250,000
Elevator, Steam Heat, Hot and Cold Water and Electric Lighted Throughout
Telephone Connections in all Rooms
42 Rooms, Completed January 1, 1907   J. F. DOUGLAS, Manager

Ad from the Nevada State Gazetteer in 1907-1908. The artist's rendition pictures a hotel building that did not resemble any actual structure.

Plans to build a third hotel, a three-story wooden building, were announced with a proposal of 123 rooms, restaurant, kitchen and lobby with special attention given to fireproofing the building. The owners planned to spend an estimated $80,000 - $90,000 to construct the new structure.

Confusing to later researchers is a listing and ad for the Goldfield Hotel in the *Nevada State Gazetteer* for 1907-1908. The hotel is described as managed by J.F. Douglas and owned by the Goldfield Realty Company on Columbia and Crook Streets in Goldfield. The ad consists of a drawing of a five-story building stating that the hotel was completed on January 1, 1907 at a cost of $250,000.

The hotel ad boasted of an elevator, steam heat, hot and

cold running water, electric lights and telephones. This hotel was never built because the owners changed their plans and decided to construct a steel, brick, and stone building instead. The construction of the present hotel building was not begun until April 1907 and was completed in January 1908. Thus, the ad in the *Nevada Star Gazetteer* was pure fiction.

⤳ HOTEL IS A MAGNIFICENT ⤶ STRUCTURE

THE SIZE AND GRANDEUR of the current four-story Goldfield Hotel are testaments to the dreams of the original owners. Their dreams went largely unfulfilled because, except for a brief period after the hotel opened, no owner operated the hotel at a profit.

The first banquet in Gold Reef - October 11, 1908. George Holesworth is seated sixth from left. -- *Nevada Historical Society*

It all began on March 22, 1907, when the owners contracted with architect George Holesworth of the prominent Reno firm of Curtis and Holesworth for an elegant hotel. The original contract to design and build the Goldfield Hotel was for $125,000. Morrill J. Curtis and George E. Holesworth designed Morrill Hall on the University of Nevada, Reno campus; the Majestic Theater in Reno; the Mizpah Hotel and the State Bank & Trust Building in Tonopah and other important structures in the state. Holesworth was the principal architect on the Goldfield Hotel, personally supervising the construction of the building.

Excavation of the basement of the hotel began in April 1907. The first floor of the opulent hotel was constructed of granite from Rocklin, California, while the upper floors were red brick. It took a little more than a year to build the U-shaped 180 foot by 100 foot four-story structure, the largest building in town. The original design included 150 sleeping rooms, and 45 suites with bathrooms, but the exact number of rooms that were built is not known. There are reports of 154 rooms to more than 200 rooms.

The hotel boasted the latest amenities, such as, steam heat and its own power plant. An electric elevator ran at 300 feet a minute, allegedly one of the fastest in Nevada, or so claimed the owners. They bragged that the building was fire proof because the hotel was outfitted with numerous metal fire escapes from the upper stories.

Looking north the front of Goldfield Hotel when under construction on November 15, 1907. -- *Nevada Historical Society*

Hotel visitors entered the lobby by climbing up a few steps from Columbia Street onto the pillared porch. The floors of the main public rooms and the entry porch were covered with small white mosaic tiles interspersed with a few black ones creating a geometric design.

There were balconies above the porch on the second and third floors from which the guests overlooked the street, town and countryside. During this time, Goldfield boasted of all the modern conveniences, such as electric lights, telephone and telegraph services, railroads, banks, newspapers, and stock exchanges. The Red Light District was located in the middle of town on Main Street, only a few blocks from the Goldfield Hotel.

Red light district located two blocks from the Goldfield Hotel.

Dark mahogany paneling covered the walls of the lobby, saloon, and dining room. Around the lobby's three iron pillars were circular, black leather buttoned banquettes; other furniture included big leather swivel chairs, couches, and strategically placed brass spittoons. Above the banquettes hung crystal electric lights, and other lights were suspended around the lobby from the beamed ceiling. The lobby housed the switchboard, a public telephone booth, the elevator and the mahogany reception desk with key rack behind it.

Lobby of the Goldfield Hotel. -- *Nevada Historical Society*

Registration desk in the lobby of the Goldfield Hotel decorated for Christmas in 1926. -- *Nevada Historical Society*

A colonnade separated the lobby from the writing room where the guests sat at carved oak desks. To the left of the lobby, the male guests entered the saloon where the piano tinkled music most nights. The men entered the dining room directly from the saloon, but the ladies used  a separate entrance from the lobby because they were not allowed in the saloon.

The dining room, frequently called the Grill, was the largest room in the building, extending the width of the building with plate glass windows that overlooked Crook Street. Enormous plants sat in the large, deep window sills. Diners could choose tables for two along the windows or round tables scattered around the floor between the columns in the room. In back of the lobby off the dining room was the kitchen, and off the right side of the lobby were two small offices used by the administrative staff of the hotel.

Top: **Blueprint drawings** of some of the hotel lobby furniture.
-- *Nevada Historical Society*

Bottom: **Goldfield Hotel** dining room. -- *Nevada Historical Society*

The month before the Grand Opening of the hotel in June 1908, the owners, unhappy with the architect's work, filed a lawsuit against Holesworth over faulty construction and cost overruns. The hotel had been in operation for five months, so the owners knew of certain problems with the building. They complained that the hot and cold water were neither, the heating system was not built to specifications, the lobby and dining room floors quivered when one person walked across them which caused a crack in the mosaic tile floor, excessive lumber was used in the construction of the hotel, lumber and plaster were purchased in excess of the market price, the owners had lost use and income from the hotel, and other contract related deficiencies.

The owners claimed that the construction costs exceeded $300,000. The actual cost of the hotel construction, however, is unclear. On later tax returns, the building was reported to have cost $337,500 to build.

The furnishings for the hotel came at an additional cost, and were as opulent as the building itself. In the beginning, manager and part owner Frank Douglas furnished only the main and second floors. He furnished the guest rooms impressively with carpeting, telephones, draperies, glass lamps, hardwood dressers with glass plate mirrors, cuspidors, and brass beds covered with woolen blankets woven with the words "Goldfield Hotel." Some of the rooms were furnished with rocking chairs or straight-backed chairs, small tables, and wardrobes. Shipped by railroad from Chicago, the hotel furniture cost about $40,000.

In addition to the furnishings, most of the rooms shared a claw foot bathtub and toilet, but all the rooms had running water. Only a few of the guest rooms were located on the main floor; most of the guest rooms were on the upper floors. In later years, the hotel employees slept in these main floor rooms, rather than guests.

⇒ MINERS' STRIKE DISRUPTS ⇐
TOWN AND HOTEL

THE GOLDFIELD HOTEL was originally scheduled to open December 25, 1907, and The Grill in the hotel advertised a Christmas Dinner menu for $15.00. Because of a bitter labor dispute in town, the owners delayed opening the hotel. On

Miner Union Hall where the miners meet. They struck in November of 1907 when the mine owner paid the miners in script, not cash.
-- *Nevada Historical Society*

November 27, 1907 after the mine owners started paying the miners' wages in script, not cash, the miners' union called a strike. Next, the mine owners further reduced wages and refused to rehire the striking union miners.

On December 3, 1907, George Wingfield convinced Governor John Sparks to wire President Theodore Roosevelt to send federal troops to Goldfield to quell any unrest and Roosevelt did. Wingfield claimed that the troops were needed to save the town from violence and destruction of property.

The soldiers arrived by train from San Francisco on December 7. Then, Roosevelt sent in a special commission to investigate the situation in Goldfield. Based on its report, he told Sparks that conditions did not support the use of federal troops and that peacekeeping was the state's duty. Roosevelt threatened that he would withdraw the troops at the end of December if Sparks did not call a special session of the legislature to pass a bill creating a state police. That law was enacted on January 29, 1908. Federal troops gradually withdrew from Goldfield starting in January, and the state police were completely in charge of the town by March 7. Ultimately, the mines reopened in January 1908, using laborers from out of state.

Soldiers' barracks where federal troops were housed during the miners strike.
-- *Nevada Historical Society*

⟾ Fruitless Dreams of Gold ⟽

The hotel "informally" opened on January 15, 1908 with 650 guests visiting the establishment while the Professor James Voss string orchestra played. The dinner menu in The Grill featured Blue Point on Half Shell, Canapé of Caviar, Soup a la Reine, Striped Bass a la Joinville with Potatoes Parisian, Filet Mignon de Beauf (sic) with Mushrooms, Roast Squab Chicken with Potatoes Juliene (sic), Goldfield Nurseries Lettuce, French Dressing, Asparagus, Brown Butter, English Pudding, Neapolitan Ice Cream, Fruits, Nuts, Raisins, Cheese and Café Noir, all for $2.00 a plate.

The actual Grand Opening of the hotel took place in June 1908. The hotel owners arranged for Pullman cars to transport guests to Goldfield from San Francisco without changing trains for the opening. At the Train Depot were dozens of taxis waiting to whisk the arrivals to the hotel.

> **George Wingfield**, as a young man, was one of the most powerful men in Goldfield. Wingfield owned the majority of the stock in the Goldfield Hotel from 1908 to 1923. Along with U.S. Senator George Nixon, Wingfied owned the Goldfield Consolidated Mines Company and controlled most of the mining and milling in the area. -- *Nevada Historical Society*

Later that year in December, George Wingfield became the majority owner of the hotel. He and Casey McDannell were the owners of the Casey Hotel, while the Goldfield Realty Company owned the Goldfield Hotel. The two businesses joined forces to form the Bonanza Hotel Company. With an exchange of stock and $200,000, the Bonanza Hotel Company became the owners of both the Goldfield Hotel and the Casey Hotel. Wingfield was the major stockholder in the new company owning 170,000 shares of the 500,000 shares issued. Al Myers owned 90,000 and the other partners each owned 45,000 shares.

At the first shareholders meeting of the new Bonanza Hotel Company, Wingfield was elected president, Myers, vice president, and Frank Douglas secretary. The object of the merger was to create one first-class profitable hotel in Goldfield. McDannell was bought out, and the Casey Hotel was closed as a hotel. And, the Bonanza Hotel Company operated the Goldfield Hotel.

Eagle Drum Corps posing in front of the Goldfield Hotel with window marked "Bonanza Hotel Company", parent company of the Goldfield Hotel. -- *Nevada Historical Society*

As previously mentioned, when the town lots in Goldfield were sold in 1903, they were actually located on federal land. It was not until 1909 that the federal government officially surveyed the two-hundred-fifty blocks of the city. In 1910, as trustee for the federal government, Nevada district court judge, Theron Stevens, sold the city lots and executed more than 1,250 deeds to the squatter/buyers of the lots. More than two years after the hotel was opened for business, Stevens executed the deed to the land under the Goldfield Hotel to the Bonanza Hotel Company on April 18, 1910.

In 1911, W.H. Leathers, manager of the hotel, provided a report by letter to George Wingfield. Leathers described the U-shaped floor plan with a lobby, dining room, kitchen, bar, pool room, office, store room and eight sleeping rooms on the main floor. The upper three floors each contained forty-six sleeping rooms for a total of 146 hotel rooms. He claimed that the building cost about $330,000 to build and that the furnishings cost about $50,000.

In the December 1911 annual report to the Bonanza Hotel Company stockholders, the profits and losses for the years 1910 and 1911 were compared. The 1910 figures show the average monthly profit of $1,290.88, while the 1911 figures show an average monthly profit of $235.42. August 1911 was the last month in that year that the hotel showed a profit.

As difficult as it was to turn a profit on the hotel, Wingfield suffered another loss. In 1912, the hotel manager, J.W. Peirce, embezzled about $5,731, apparently, by pocketing the cash from the bar, cigar stand and other hotel businesses.

Wingfield was luckier the next year because the hotel escaped physical damage from the flash flood on September 13, 1913. Most of the town and the Goldfield Hotel located on high ground were untouched. Others suffered grave misfortune. Two women lost their lives, Eulalia Robles and Olive De Garmo. And, the train yard located in a lower part of town was heavily damaged.

From 1914 to 1917, the Bonanza Hotel Company financial reports for the Goldfield Hotel and for the Casey Hotel, then rented out for offices, showed some profitable months and some months when the company lost money with more months showing a loss than a profit. Wingfield operated the hotel until 1917 when he began leasing the entire building to others to operate, beginning with R. L. Wanger for $400 a month.

In 1920, Wingfield announced his decision to close the hotel, and remove the plumbing and window frames to ship them to Winnemucca for installation in the proposed new Humboldt Hotel. In response, A. G. Cummings, on behalf of some Chicago capitalists, who owned a large interest in the nearby Montezuma mining claim, paid $5,000 down to purchase an option on the hotel. Some mining companies and local residents believed that the closure of the hotel would be detrimental to their mining claims and the town, so they formed the Goldfield Improvement Association. They raised $25,500 for about half interest in the hotel stock, and Wingfield decided to keep the hotel open.

Goldfield flood on September 13, 1913. Eulalia Robles and Olive De Garmo died. -- *Nevada Historical Society*

Wingfield continued to lease the Goldfield Hotel to a long line of businessmen for various amounts between $200 and $600 a month until 1923. Then, the Elko hotelman Newton Crumley rented the hotel for $400 a month. No stranger to the Central Nevada area, Newt Crumley had lived in nearby Tonopah,

Nevada during the boom years in the early 1900s and in 1919.

Wingfield sold the Bonanza Hotel Company, including the Goldfield Hotel, to Crumley shortly after a major fire swept through Goldfield on July 6, 1923. That fire started across the street from the hotel and ultimately destroyed 100 homes and 25 blocks of the commercial section of the city. The windows in the hotel broke due to the intensity of the heat. A piece of hot metal flew through a third floor window and landed on a bed which caught fire. Fortunately, the guest was in the room and quickly extinguished the fire.

The property loss in town was estimated at $1 million, most of which was not insured. Within weeks of the fire, one third of the population moved out of Goldfield because mining jobs were scarce. The town never recovered. Then, another fire swept the town on September 29,

Newton Crumley, the elder, probably during the time he owned the Goldfield Hotel in the 1920s.
-- *Frances Crumley Collection*

1924 destroying the buildings remaining in the commercial section of town. The report was that many of the commercial buildings were built of limestone. The heat from the fire made the water in the limestone evaporate, and the buildings collapsed because the stones turned to dust. Fortunately, the Goldfield Hotel

Aftermath of fire that destroyed most of the town of Goldfield in 1923.
-- *Nevada Historical Society*

was constructed of brick and granite, so neither of these two fires harmed the hotel.

Apparently, Newton Crumley was not interested in turning a profit from running the hotel; he had other uses for the property. He filed three mining claims named the Goldfield Hotel #1, Goldfield Hotel #2, and Goldfield Hotel #3 when he owned the building. The current Goldfield Hotel building and its predecessors were built over the shaft of the Vera Lode, a mining claim of The Doctor White Wolf Mining Company, filed on March 2, 1904.

Two men sitting on the mine dump behind the Goldfield Hotel during the hotel's construction.
-- *Nevada Historical Society*

The mine shaft in the basement of the hotel must have been obvious when Crumley operated the hotel because it is still visible today. If he explored the tunnel, his mining results could not have been successful because he sold the hotel to Joseph Basile, Jr., in June

1925. And, Crumley concentrated his efforts in Elko where he owned the Commercial Hotel.

During Crumley's ownership of the hotel, he continued Wingfield's policy of leasing parts of the hotel to other businesses, including the hotel dining room. Marko Dobroslavich leased the restaurant part of the hotel from both Wingfield, Crumley and later owners. Dobroslavich started as an employee of the hotel after he arrived in Goldfield from Dubrovnik (Austria and later known as Yugoslavia) in 1911, not speaking a word of English. His first job was washing dishes in the Goldfield Hotel seven days a week on 12 hour shifts for $2 a day plus room and board. He quickly learned how to cook, saved his money, and bought the restaurant for $1,100 in 1918.

White linen tablecloths and napkins and sterling silver cutlery graced the tables. He offered a variety of foods, including fish, duck, rabbit, frog legs from San Francisco, bear meat and fresh vegetables grown in Fish Lake Valley, Nevada. Twenty-three years after buying the restaurant Dobroslavich, one of the hotel's few success stories, walked away from his business leaving the silver, linen and dishes on the tables, when the hotel closed in 1938.

⇒ HOTEL IS IN THE DOLDRUMS ⇐

DURING DOBROSLAVICH'S LEASE, the ownership of the hotel changed hands a couple of times in the 1930s. All the new owners were from California. A series of mortgages were recorded on the property. James Belden purchased the hotel from Joseph Basile, Jr., and recorded a mortgage for $105,000 on November 6, 1925. On the same day Belden also mortgaged the hotel with Henry Windt for $50,000 and with James A. Nolan for $12,000. Joseph Basile, Jr., transferred his Beldon mortgage to J.V. Nelson in June 1926. And, the Belden/Nolan mortgage was paid off in 1930.

On April 15, 1930, J.V. Nelson and Estella W. Nelson executed a deed to the hotel to G.J. Landers and Anna Joyce Landers. On the same day, the G.J. Landers and Anna Joyce Landers assigned their interest in the Goldfield Hotel to J.V. Nelson and Estella W. Nelson for the $15,000 they owned the Nelsons. The Landers obtained good title to the property, and on May 14, 1930, the Landers executed a deed to Mable Hartman.

The hotel was operated without much fanfare or publicity, but the property was generating some revenues because Hartman filed a Notice of Claim against the Nelsons for $424.80 for the hotel rent their manager had collected and had not paid to Hartman, as required by the escrow agreement between the parties.

One of the busiest couple of weeks at the hotel in the early 1930s occurred during the blizzard of January 1933. One famous Nevada hotel guest, thanks to the storm, was United States Senator-elect Pat McCarran, on his way to Las Vegas accompanied by M.C. Kloskey, a mining engineer. They got stuck in the snow about eight miles from Goldfield on the Tonopah highway. Their car had to be towed to town, where they left it because the road to Las Vegas remained blocked by the snow for two weeks, long after they took the train back to Reno.

Meanwhile, they joined about 40 others who were stranded during the blizzard. McCarran entertained the other guests with his views on mining in Nevada. It was the first time he met Eva Adams. Apparently, they were equally impressed with each other because she later became his Office Administrator in Washington D.C., and afterwards she was appointed Director of the U.S. Mint.

A few years later the hotel was sold again. According to the *Reno Evening Gazette*, July 4, 1936, the hotel was sold two days before by Mettie Jones of Long Beach, California, to mining man Ray Holbrook of Goldfield and L.F. Detwiler, and Ray French. Holbrook and his wife were to manage the property. They planned to renovate the hotel and restore it to its former glory as a meeting place for the community as well as a haven for travelers, but their operation did not last long. In September 1938, the Holbrooks closed the doors of the hotel.

⌐ ARMY REVIVES THE HOTEL ⌐

IN JANUARY 1942, the property was purchased in the name of Arthur E. Grey, owner of a large plumbing business in Los Angeles, California. Apparently, there were other California partners, and the front man for the group was Benjamin Brodsky. He described their scheme to convert Goldfield into a playground for the wealthy, suggesting that the hotel would become the "Monte Carlo of America." They planned to spend about $100,000 to remodel the first and second floors. Delicate, modern wallpaper with floral designs was installed in the guests rooms, and the woodwork was painted light grey and off-white. Later, when the number of hotel residents increased to 150 people, the upper floors were renovated.

Soldiers in the street in front of the hotel after a 1943 snow storm. -- *Central Nevada Historical Society, Martha Reiley Goodrich collection*

In February, the hotel owners announced that the company had purchased a 40 to 50-seat bus to transport the airmen and mechanics from the Tonopah Army Air Field to the hotel. In October the owners reported that the hotel was accommodating between 25 and 40 people a night, mostly officers and their families from the Tonopah Army Air Field.

Despite the renovations, the hotel was not the luxurious

place it had once been. According to Beverly Duffy, when she, her husband Lt. Pat Duffy and their baby son, moved into the hotel, even though the hotel's steam heat was functional, the lobby was boarded up to keep the cold wind out. The ornate elevator of black and gold grilled iron was not operational, and the elevator cage was filled with old white china chamber pots and matching wash bowls.

The lobby, called the waiting room, was filled with couches and comfortable chairs, a writing desk, lamps and a baby grand piano. Off the waiting room to the right was the billiard room with glass paneled doors. Across the lobby was the light blue saloon with a mahogany bar and a long mirrored back bar with shelves holding glasses and a few old bottles.

The base sent double feature movies over to the hotel on Wednesday nights. The cost of admission was 50 cents and the whole town was invited to watch the movies in the saloon. Large wood sliding doors opened from the saloon into the dining room. Even though the hotel had advertised the dining room, the restaurant was not opened for service.

Their room at the front of the hotel was small, but included a bathroom complete with a claw foot bathtub. The Duffys cooked in their room on a hot plate, eating one dish meals. They stored their food and dishes in apple crates and also used the crates to hold their hot plate and coffee pot. And, the hotel furnished their bed linens and towels.

Later on, the Duffys moved into a large suite with French doors leading out to their own private balcony. Duffy claimed that they had a great view of the desert. That room's antique furniture included a mahogany desk, two chairs, dresser and a brass bed. The bathroom also had a claw foot bathtub they kept ice in during the summer to keep their food, milk and beer cold. During the winter, they stored their food on the iron fire escape to keep it cold.

When the airmen left Tonopah after World War II ended, the hotel permanently closed in September 1945. It was the last time the hotel housed paying guests.

⮞ HOTEL LANGUISHES UNDER ⮜
NEW OWNERS

IN FEBRUARY 1955, the hotel was sold to the Las
Vegas Investment Corporation. The principals of the corporation
were Maurice Selman and A.F. Selman, from Beverly Hills,
California. They hired Harold Lankford to remodel the hotel, but
the only reported
improvement made was
to replace the roof.

Harolds Club billboard situated next
to the Goldfield Hotel on Crook Street.

Without
apparently reopening the
hotel, the Selmans
entered into a five-year
lease option to sell the
hotel to Clark Feeley,
John Douglas, and Daryl
Jorgenson in November
1974. Douglas and
Feeley were card dealers, while Jorgenson was in hotel
management - all from Las Vegas, Nevada. They had ambitious
plans to not only open the hotel but also to open a bar, casino and
museum to take advantage of the charter bus trade. They even
discussed air flights into Goldfield. In addition, they purchased
several other pieces of property in Goldfield, including a school
building, a mining office and eighty town lots. During that time
Harolds Club had its famous, "Harolds Club or Bust" signs all
over the world, including in the vacant lot next to the Goldfield
Hotel.

⇐ Mythomania About the Hotel ⇒

DURING THIS PERIOD promoters of the town and owners of the hotel began circulating stories that were not supported by facts about the hotel's history. For example, in May 1971, the caretaker of the hotel, Arthur Trevor, told a *S.F. Examiner & Chronicle* reporter that two U.S. Presidents had stayed at the hotel, although he did not name them. Trevor also claimed that Jack Dempsey, the boxer, worked there as a bouncer. Both stories were tall tales. Dempsey was no stranger to Goldfield. He fought there at the Hippodrome. As for being a bouncer, in Dempsey's autobiography, he stated, "I never was a saloon bouncer in my life."

Then, on November 1, 1974, the new owners of the hotel, Clark Feeley, John Douglas and Daryl Jorgenson were quoted in the *Las Vegas Sun* claiming that Wyatt Earp dealt a few rounds of cards at the hotel. This claim is also a tall tale. It is true that Virgil Earp, his brother, was an Esmeralda County deputy sheriff. According to newspaper reports, Wyatt traveled to Goldfield to visit his brother Virgil in February 1905. Wyatt, accompanied by his wife, stopped in Bull Frog to check out their mining claims there before venturing on the Goldfield. Apparently, Wyatt had explored the Goldfield area a few years before and did not believe the place had a future. Except for this brief visit, apparently Wyatt had no other connections to the town, despite the stories otherwise. Furthermore, the current Goldfield Hotel, of course, was not built until 1908, so it would have been impossible for Wyatt Earp to deal cards there in 1905.

The tallest tale these Las Vegas owners told was that the interior and exterior of the hotel looked exactly as it did during the Gans-Nelson prizefight that was held in 1906. That was impossible because the groundbreaking for the current the hotel began in 1907, seven months after the fight, so the hotel could not have looked exactly like it did in 1906.

The final story these same owners began was that the lobby ceiling was covered in 22 carat gold. In the February 2, 1975 *Nevada State Journal*, one of the new owners claimed they were rejuvenating the 22 carat gold leaf lobby ceiling because the paint was peeling. No records could be found to support this claim, nor after inspection of the building is there any evidence that the ceiling was covered with gold. The actual material in the ceiling was not reported at the time the hotel was built. It stands to reason that if the ceiling had been covered in gold, the original owners would have listed it in their promotional materials. The 22 carat gold ceiling is another myth about the Goldfield Hotel.

≈ CAMPERS AND GHOSTS ≈
IN THE HOTEL

THE NEXT BUYERS CAME ALONG in the 1970s. According to *But You Can't Leave, Shirley* by Shirley A. Porter (Dybicz), she and her husband Dennis Dybicz fell in love with the hotel when they drove by it. They paid $25,000 for the property and formed a limited partnership with Great Western Company of California and others to finance their purchase of the hotel property. These transactions gave them access to the hotel where they camped out in the hotel with Porter's two youngest daughters.

At the time they lived there (late 1978 to 1981), the hotel completely lacked any amenities, no functioning plumbing, heating or electricity in the building. They made a few minor repairs to the building, but were without funds to make the substantial repairs that were needed to make the hotel operational.

In her book Porter described what was left of the original mine shaft and boarded up area in the basement filled with water and rocks. She and her husband removed some of the rocks and attempted to explore the old shaft without much success.

Porter was the first to describe the hotel's ghosts. Apparently, she was acquainted with several ghosts, but the more significant ghosts were the man walking above the dining room, she named him, "Mr. G" and a young girl, tall and slender, with blond hair dressed in a blue-green dress who haunted room 109 on the ground floor. Later some people named this ghost, "Gertie," while others called her, "Elizabeth."

It appeared to Porter that the girl was struggling to get out of the room. Porter concluded she had been held in the room against her will and chained to the radiator. There are several theories about this ghost. One story was that she was pregnant by a married man, so she killed herself after her father locked her up in the room. Another story was that after she gave birth to her baby in the room, she was left to die or was murdered. The newborn baby was thrown down the mine shaft in the basement of the hotel and is often heard crying in the night.

Another version of the story is that she was chained to the radiator by George Wingfield because it was his baby. This story seems unlikely because he would have been able to escape any liability for any misconduct by virtue of his position in the community. For example, May Baric, Wingfield's common law wife, filed against him for a divorce, and although everyone knew they lived together as Mr. and Mrs. Wingfield from 1902 to 1906, he was successful in having the case decided in his favor with May Baric ordered to pay his legal fees. Since Wingfield was above the law in Goldfield, he would never have had to resort to chaining a woman to a radiator because he impregnated her.

Others have reported that George Wingfield is also a ghost, usually sensed on the lobby staircase. Some have stated they could smell his cigar smoke, and there is a report that cigar ashes were found in the fuse box that had been unopened for 50 years.

In recent years, numerous hotel visitors taking photographs with digital cameras had seen unexplained orbs of lights in their pictures taken in different rooms in the hotel. Other visitors had felt sudden rushes of cold air on their necks. They claim these images and air movements support their theory that the hotel is haunted.

Porter and Dybiczs' sojourn in the hotel did not last long. Their majority partner in the General Western Corporation, Lester

O'Shea, a San Francisco entrepreneur and real estate tycoon, asked or told them to leave the premises in 1981. At that time O'Shea had acquired controlling interest in the hotel for about $450,000.

≈ ANOTHER ILL-FATED GEM ≈
OF THE DESERT

LIKE PORTER, AFTER LESTER O'SHEA drove by the property, he too succumbed to the siren's call to own the hotel. At the time he purchased the building, it was about 70 years old and had been closed for more than 30 years. Initially, O'Shea spent $50,000 replacing the roof, while he searched for a hotel chain to help market the hotel. The major improvement he made to the building was to jack up, stabilize and retrofit the building against earthquakes. Reno architect Roger Biale was hired to perform the architectural and engineering studies to ensure that the building was earthquake proof.

Critical to O'Shea's expenditures on the hotel were the federal tax credits available for restoration of old buildings. He worked successfully with the Nevada State Historic Preservation Office to have the central part of Goldfield where the hotel is located declared a National Register historic district.

O'Shea spared no expense on renovating the building. He hired architect Tom Taylor from California to design the restoration of the hotel, to bring the building up to the electrical and plumbing codes, and to install a sprinkler system and air-conditioning system. The design included adding a bathroom to each room reducing the number of guest rooms. The plans included a new kitchen, museum, gift shop and cocktail lounge.

Resource Development Co., of Sparks, Nevada, was awarded the construction contract to complete the remodeling by

January 1988. There were plans for repairing the ornate elevator in the lobby. The O'Sheas claimed that Otis Elevator Co., had agreed to donate up to $250,000 in parts and labor to repair the elevator. Camille, Lester's wife, stated she hoped to enclose the working parts in glass, so the guests could watch the elevator in operation.

Stories that the hotel elevator was the first electric elevator built west of the Mississippi is another tale that is often repeated. This tale about the elevator first appeared in newspaper articles in the 1970s. According to Guy Rocha, Nevada State Archivist, in his search of the Otis Elevator company archives, the first elevator west of the Mississippi was installed in Spokane, Washington in 1890.

In the newspaper articles when the hotel opened and in later accounts, the only mention of the hotel elevator is that the hotel had one. In one of the first promotional pieces on the hotel, the owners bragged that the elevator ran at 300 feet a minute, making it the fastest elevator in the state. Obviously, if their claim was it was the fastest, clearly the owners knew there were other elevators in Nevada, west of the Mississippi, at that time.

Another often repeated tale about the hotel is that President Theodore Roosevelt spoke from one of the hotel balconies. Lester O'Shea claimed that the hotel maintained a spacious suite just for occasional visits by President Roosevelt. According to Phil Earl, Curator of History Emeritus at the Nevada Historical Society, there was a man who posed as the president at various functions on the day of the famous 42-round Gans-Nelson bout on September 3, 1906. At the time the people knew the truth, but later historians did not recognize the spoof. Additionally, the current hotel was not built until 1908, two years after the Gans-Nelson fight. Even, the second Hotel Goldfield opened a month after the fight and was a wooden structure without any balconies, so it would have been impossible for Roosevelt to speak from one of the hotel's balconies.

In the O'Sheas' ambitious plans for the hotel, they included a 24-hour coffee shop with seating for 200 people and later on, they planned to add a swimming pool and convention center. Lester also planned to apply for a gaming license, so he hired Don McGhie, a Reno accountant specializing in gaming, to do a feasibility study on the property and his wife, Wallis, to design the future casino. Later, O'Shea hired gaming authority, Gary Royer to do an economic study of the property. O'Shea expected to put 70 to 100 slot machines, a roulette wheel and possibly a faro (card) game in the lobby with blackjack available in the bar.

Brochure the O'Sheas used to promote the hotel in the 1980s.

In anticipation of opening the hotel on July 1, 1988, they hired staff, ordered furniture and booked room reservations. His wife, Camille, said the couple was counting on a strong bus business, as well as other tourists, especially from Canada, Japan and Europe.

Unfortunately, O'Sheas abandoned the hotel renovations and the hotel never reopened. According to Lester, the national economy worsened and interest rates shot up to 18% making it impossible to borrow money. He claimed he spent $4 million on restoring the building, and their partner, Louis Aubert, failed to invest the $2 million he had promised. The property sat empty for years. Finally, on May 2, 1995, the Esmeralda County Treasurer filed a tax deed taking title to the property for failure to pay property taxes on the hotel. Then, the title to the property was tied up in bankruptcy proceedings delaying the county from taking title to the property until June 2003.

NEW DREAMS OF GLORY

TODAY, THE LIVELIEST and best preserved ghost town in Nevada is Goldfield, and among the best preserved building in town is the Goldfield Hotel. Located in a three to four square mile historic district, the hotel has been purchased once again. The new owner, Edger "Red" Roberts, paid $360,000 to the Esmeralda County Clerk for the title to the hotel at the county tax auction in August 2003. From Northern Nevada, Roberts plans to renovate the basement and main floor of the hotel intending to reopen the hotel in August 2005. Time will tell if he will succeed in reversing the hotel's fortunes by creating a true gem in the desert, or will he too find that the Goldfield Hotel is only fools' gold?

myths, 32-33, 38

Nelson, J. V. and Estella W., 27

Nevada Historical Society, 38

Nevada State Historic
Preservation Office, 37

Nevada State Gazetteer, 10-11

Nevada State Journal, 33

Nixon, George, 20

Nixon-Wingfield building, 2

Nolan, James, 27

O'Shea, Lester and Camile, 35-39

Otis Elevator Company. See
elevator

owners. See hotel owners

Paiute, 5

Peirce, J. W., 22

Porter, (Dybicz) Shirley A., 34-37

Preston, Morrie, 9

Red Light District, 14

Reno Evening Gazette, 28

Reno, 2, 39

Resources Development Co., 37

Rice, George Graham, 7

Rickard, Tex, 7

Roberts, Edger "Red", 40

Robles, Eulalia, 22-23

Rocha, Guy, 38

Roosevelt, Theodore, 18-19, 38

Rosenthal, Ben, 7

Royer, Gary, 39

"Sandstorm," 4

San Francisco, 19-20, 36

Selman, Maurice, and A. F., 31

*San Francisco Examiner &
Chronicle*, 32

Shoshone, 5

Smith, John, 9

Smith, Joseph, 9

snow storm, 29. See also blizzard

Sparks, Governor John, 18-19

Sparks, 37

State Bank and Trust Company, 8,
12

Stevens, Theron, 22

Stimler, Harry, 4-5

Taylor, Tom, 37

Tonopah, 5, 23, 28-30

Tonopah Army Air Field, 29

train, 20, 22

Trevor, Arthur, 32

University of California, 8-9

University of Nevada, 12

Vera Lode, 25

Wanger, R. L., 23

Waugh and Henningson, 9

Windt, Henry, 27

Wingfield, George, 7, 18, 20-24,
26, 35

Eastern Slope Publisher
P.O. Box 20357
Reno, Nevada 89515-0357
775/825-2694
775/825-8594 fax

ORDER FORM

THE
GOLDFIELD
HOTEL

Gem of the Desert

Please send to:

Name: _____

Address: _____

City: _____ State: _____ Zip Code: _____

Telephone: _____ (If we have questions about your order).

Quantity _____ @ $9.95/each: $_____

Shipping and Handling: $ 2.00/each book $_____

Nevada Residents: Sales Tax $0.73/each book $_____

Total Enclosed $_____